CONTENTS

To Anna Fiorenza and Mara

THE CONFUSED ME

This man is looking confused because battling inside him two very different personalities are trying to take control of his life.

During the day he is Dr Jekyll, a hard working physician who spends his time doing respectable things like pre-scribing aspirins, feeling puls-es, peering down ears, look-ing up noses, knocking knees with a hammer, sticking spoons down throats, instructing patients to cough, and telling them things like, **'I don't really know what's wrong with you but it's probably a virus and the chances are that it will clear up within a week**.'

However, at night, after retreating to his secret laboratory and drinking a brew of steaming, bubbling chemicals, he turns into Mr Hyde, a hideous looking creature with hair sprouting from every part of his body, blood dripping from his mouth and fingers, who spends his time lurking in shadowy streets and alleyways doing disrespectable things like murdering young women.

Now, unfortunately, this man has a '**GOOD TIME**' being both characters (although of course in different ways). But he knows that one of them will have to go because the battle between them is too painful to live with. His problem, then, is deciding which 'good time' he prefers and therefore which character should stay and be the person he calls '**ME**'.

THE BATTLE INSIDE ME

Many people believe that all human beings have the same sorts of problems as this man. They are not suggesting, of course, that we drink strange potions, turn hideously ugly and become psychopaths. However, they are saying that inside each of us there is also a battle raging between different personalities, and so, like this man, we also end up behaving as if we were totally different people.

They also suggest that, like this man, we also often have a '**GOOD TIME**' being these different characters and therefore have problems deciding which characters should go or stay. In other words, deciding which personality battling inside us should win the battle and be the personality we call '**ME**'.

The following poem describes this battle:

There is a wolf in me ... fangs pointed for tearing gashes ... a red tongue for raw meat ... and the hot lapping of blood ... There is a fox in me ... a silver grey fox ... I sniff and guess ... I pick things out of the air ... I nose in the night ... I circle and loop and double-cross.
There is a hog in me .... a snout and a belly ... a machinery for eating and grunting ... a machinery for sleeping satisfied ... in the sun ...
There is a a baboon in me ... clambering-clawed ... dog-faced ... yawmping a gallot's hunger ... hairy under the armpits ... ready to snarl and kill.
There is an eagle in me and a mockingbird ... and the eagle flies among the Rocky mountains of my dreams ... and the mockingbird warbles in the early forenoon before the dew is gone.
(From The Circus Within Me by Carl Sandburg.)

1   In your own words explain the decision that Dr Jekyll felt he had to make and why he found it so difficult.

2   Some people believe that all human beings face the same sort of decision as Dr Jekyll. What do they mean? Do you agree? Give reasons for your answer.

3   In the poem the writer is suggesting that in him there is a battle going on between different animals. Try to explain what characteristics each of the animals represent in the poet .

4   Draw a line down the middle of a plain piece of paper. On one side of the paper write the title 'How I am when I'm at school' and on the other write 'How I am when I'm alone'. Draw animals (or an animal) on either side to illustrate the two titles.

5   Write your own poem entitled 'The Circus Within Me' and choose animals which represent the different characteristics within you which are battling for control.

6   Many people say there have been occasions when they have not felt in control of their behaviour, i.e. as if some wild animal within them has taken control. Have you ever felt that some wild animal within you took control of your behaviour? Give details.

7   Which animals within you would you like to disappear from your life, and which to stay? Give reasons for your answer.

8   A man called Paul decribes the battle going on inside him in a different way. Read Romans 8:14-25 and in your own words explain what he is saying.

9   Is your experience of yourself similar to that of Paul? Give reasons for your answer.

BE A DOG

If you want to have a really '**GOOD TIME**' in life, then you need to get what you **want** when you **wan**t it. Now, since we live in a world where what you want is usually what everybody else wants, this means that, to have a 'good time', you will have to behave like a dog. Not of course like a toy Poodle, a cuddly Pekinese or a hairless Chihuahua, but more like a Neapolitan mastiff, a Pit Bull Terrier, a Dobermann or an Alsatian. These are fighting dogs with bites far worse than their barks who will tear other dogs to pieces in order to get what they want. And if you want to get what you want and enjoy life that's how you should behave. In other words, work out what you **want** in life, work out how to get it and then be prepared to fight viciously for whatever it may be.

Now, this may mean doing things like cheating, lying, stealing, ripping people off, putting people down, humiliating or flattering them, framing them, breaking promises, spreading rumours, revealing secrets, head-butting ... and worse.

But don't hold back. Remember, in a '**dog eat dog world**' it's important to get in the first bite, because if you don't, someone else will.

But if we all behaved like wild dogs, life would turn into a never-ending fight and not even the most vicious dogs would enjoy that sort of life!

Well that's like saying that you shouldn't build a bridge because if everybody stood on it at the same time it would collapse. The point is that not everybody in the world would – and neither would everybody behave like a fighting dog.

Most people, in fact, behave like weak-willed, small-minded sheep, huddling together for safety, doing what they are told and bleating at the first sign of danger. So, those who choose the '**DOG LIFE**' will not always be fighting but will spend most of their time enjoying life at the expense of those who choose to live timidly.

So, live like Alexander the Great, Julius Caesar and Napoleon. These are the great '**fighting dogs**' of history who saw what they wanted, worked out how to get it and were prepared to do whatever was necessary to acquire it, even if this meant treading over the lives of thousands of other human beings. They were not held back by things like conscience or other people's disapproval. What they 'wanted' was all that mattered and that's why they all ended up with what they wanted and having such a great time.

1   The boy in this section believes that if we want the best possible life then we should live **self**-centred lives by allowing the 'wild dog' inside of us to gain control of our lives. Explain his reasons for saying this.

2   The girl objected to this advice. In your own words explain her reasons for doing so.

3   How did the boy reply to her objections?

4   Does the 'wild dog' inside you ever gain control of your life? Give some examples or reasons why not.

5   When the 'wild dog' is unleashed in your life do you enjoy life more? Give reasons for your answer.

6   Over 2,500 years ago a philosopher called Plato wrote a book called The Republic. The book contains conversations between a man called Socrates (who objected to the 'wild dog'

theory of life) and those who supported it. Below are the views of a supporter called Thrasymachus:

'I'm afraid you're very simple-minded, Socrates. You ought to consider how the just man always comes off worse than the unjust. For instance, in any business relations between them, you won't find the just man better off at the end of the deal than the unjust. Again, in their   relations with the State, when there are taxes to be paid, the unjust man will pay less on the same income, and when there's anything to be got he'll get a lot, the just man nothing. So we see that injustice, given scope, has greater strength and freedom and power than justice.'

(a) In your own words, sum up the views of Thrasymachus.

(b) Do you agree with his views? Give reasons for your answer.

BE A PIG

If you want to have a really '**GOOD TIME**' in life, then you must learn (unlike the dog) to ignore those wants that may involve you in painful fights. So, behave like a pig. These animals don't go out of their way to fight with each other. They simply concentrate on satisfying those wants which give them '**PLEASURE**' and which don't involve any sort of '**PAIN**'. They spend their time then either with their snouts in the trough 'eating and drinking' or simply wallowing around in mud keeping cool and looking very laid back.

So, if you want to have a good time in life then behave just like this. Ignore those **wants** where you risk getting your head kicked in. Instead, spend your time wallowing in harmless and pleasurable activities like eating, drinking and sex. Limit   yourself to these sorts of activities and believe me, you'll have a more enjoyable life than all the wild dogs of history.

But if I take your advice and simply live for pleasure, I'll probably end up experiencing more pain than the wild dogs!

Why?

Well, if I go through life stuffing myself with food, I'll end up with a pork belly and suffering from all those diseases that come from being a glutton.

FAT PIG

Furthermore, if I spend a lot of time with my snout inside a beer glass, I'll end up with constant head-pounding hangovers, throwing up down toilets and possibly cirrhosis of the liver.

PIG SICK

And if, as you seem to suggest, I spend my time sleeping around, then apart from the possibility of producing litters of babies I'll probably end up with diseases like herpes, gonorrhoea, syphilis and perhaps even aids.

Swine!

So I can't see how a '**PIG LIFE**' will give me a '**GOOD TIME**'. As far as I can see, I'll have just as much pain as the dogs of this world, and perhaps more, if I develop a disease that ends up with me losing my bacon.

Well, you're only going to experience these sorts of pains if you 'pig' yourself in a really big way. What you need to know is when to stop hogging and drinking yourself silly.

So follow the advice of a Greek philosopher called **Epicurus** (341 BC–270 BC). He agreed that the only way to enjoy life is to fill it with '**PLEASURE**'. However, he understood that if you go wild when your snout is in the trough, then there is likely to be a pay-back time. So he taught people to enjoy life by **controlling** their appetites so that '**pleasure**' would outweigh any follow-up '**pain**' – for example, drinking wine, but not the whole bottle; eating good food but not in excess; and participating in sex but not like a rabbit. In other words, to behave like a '**PIG**' but not a '**GREEDY PIG**'.

1 The girl in this section argues that if you want to have a good time you should (as with the dog) lead a self-centred life and that the best way to do this is to allow the 'pig' inside you to control your life. In your own words, explain her reasons for saying this.

2 The boy in this section disagrees. Explain his reasons for objecting to the 'pig' life.

3 What is the girl's reply to these objections?

4 Perhaps you sometimes behave like a 'pig'. If so, do you find yourself enjoying life and enjoying the person you have become?

5 Who, in your opinion, are the 'pigs' of our society? Do you think they enjoy life fully? Give reasons for your answer.

6 A philosopher called John Stuart Mill believed that we should try to live for pleasure. However, he wasn't happy with the idea that we should simply live for basic '**pig pleasures**'. He tried to explain why in the following way:

'We can imagine a pig whose life is ... filled with swinish pleasures and we can imagine a Socrates (a philosopher) whose intellectual achievements ... have resulted in the frustrating perception that his greatest achievement is to appreciate just how little he knows. The pig is satisfied (by his pleasures) Socrates dissatisfied, so (this) would appear to commend the life of the pig.'

However, Mill thought it was clear that the life of a 'dissatisfied Socrates' is better than the life of a 'satisfied pig'. Do you agree? Give reasons for your answer.

7 John Stuart Mill tried to support his view by saying that some pleasures in life are better (higher) than others, i.e. they provide us with a greater 'quantity' and a better 'quality' of pleasure. And so things like reading philosophy, playing the piano/guitar, watching/participating in a play give us more and a higher form of pleasure than stuffing ourselves with chocolate bars, watching Coronation Street or torturing people. Do you agree? If so, make a list of pleasures with the 'highest' coming first and the 'lowest' last.

8 Look back on the list you made in question 7 and try to work out how you decided which were higher or lower pleasures.

BE A GORILLA

Well, I believe that you will only have a really '**GOOD TIME**' in life when you understand that it depends upon other people having a good time as well. So, be a '**GORILLA**'. These animals don't move around the jungle alone looking for an enjoyable time. They know that jungle life is dangerous and that on your own you'll spend most of your time watching your back and having a '**bad time**.' So instead, they live in groups where each member gives on up the idea of always **getting what they want when they want it.** Instead, they think of each other's needs. And when they do so, more of each member's own needs get satisfied because the group gives them the protection they need to live safe and contented lives.

And if you want to look after your own interests and really enjoy life then you need to behave like this. In other words, recognise (like the 'gorilla') that this world is a jungle and that roaming around it alone like a 'wild dog' is not likely to end up with you getting what you want when you want it. Instead, recognise (like the gorilla again) that you need the protection and help of the group and that you'll get more '**pleasure**' than '**pain**' in your life if you spend some of your time thinking about the interests of other people.

Which groups could I join to protect my interests?

Well first of all, you could become a loyal member of the group you call '**MY COUNTRY**' and in exchange for putting up with the hassle of obeying the law, paying taxes, voting in elections and fighting in wars, this group will provide you with things like an army, a police force, schools, hospitals, transport, a job, money and food.

Secondly, you could become a loyal member of the group you call '**MY FAMILY**' and in exchange for things like obeying your mum and dad, tolerating brothers and sisters, doing the washing-up, and being in early at the weekends, you'll get a roof over your head, heat and light, money for clothes, food on your plate and the occasional holiday.

And finally, you could become a loyal member of the group you call '**THE PEOPLE I HANG AROUND WITH**' and in exchange for things like sharing bars of chocolate, laughing at weak jokes and helping out in fights, you'll get company in the evenings and possibly even friendship.

Of course, there are many other groups you could choose to protect your interests and give you a good life (including criminal ones like the Mafia). However, whichever one you choose you will end up choosing the same basic philosophy of life, i.e. a philosophy which says that you will have the best possible life if you follow the principle of:

'**YOU SCRATCH MY BACK AND I'LL SCRATCH YOURS.**'

But this is the philosophy of the weak who huddle together in herds to protect themselves against the strong... But I'm a WILD DOG and I can get you to scratch my back for nothing, so why should I put up with the hassle of being nice to you when I can just be nice to myself at your expense?

Well, there are at least two reasons.

First of all, you can't be sure that you are the strongest animal in the jungle. Tomorrow, for example, you may come across an animal far wilder than yourself who will boss you around as you intend to do with me. There are no guarantees, then, that you will always be in a position to **get what you want when you want it**.

And secondly, even if you turn out to be the strongest and wildest animal in the jungle, there will come a time when you will grow old and lose your power and strength. Then, of course, you will be vulnerable to the power of the other dogs and will need the help of others to survive.

So take the advice of the British philosopher, **Jeremy Bentham** (1748–1832). He said that each of us is more likely to enjoy a life of '**pleasure**' if each member of society tries to create:

'**The greatest amount of pleasure and the least amount of pain for the greatest number of people**.'

1 The boy in this section also believes that you will have the best possible life if you live a self-centred life. He suggests that the best way to look after yourself is to allow the 'gorilla' in you to control your life. Explain his reasons for saying this.

2 The girl disagrees. Explain her point of view (see page 9).

3 In your own words explain the boy's reply to the girl's objections.

4 Not everybody in a group (for example a country) is able to 'scratch the backs' of the other members. What do you think would be this boy's attitude to these people?

5 (a) Think about some of the groups you belong to and write them down.

(b) Now think about the unselfish things you do in these groups and write down some examples.

(c) Finally, try to work out whether in fact you do them for selfish reasons. In other words, do you operate by the gorilla principle of '**You scratch my back and I'll scratch yours**' and do these things so that one day you will get something from the group for yourself (even if it is praise)?

6 Some people argue that all human beings act selfishly, even when they appear to be acting selflessly. For example, those who appear to be making sacrifices in order to work amongst the poor and sick in dangerous situations do so because they get a selfish kick out of working like this. Do you agree that all human action is basically selfish?

7 Can you think of any behaviour, either your own or others you know which may not have been powered by the principle of '**what's in it for me?**'

RESEARCH

8 Teachers often appear to be selfless members of school communities. For example, they sometimes take after school clubs, give up evenings to meet parents and spend some of their holidays on school trips. Interview a teacher(s) and try to find out whether they came into teaching for selfless reasons and whether giving up their free time in school has nothing to do with the principle of 'what's in it for me?' (e.g. promotion, good reference etc). Make up your own questionnaire.

BE A CHAMELEON

The world is a jungle full of wild animals all out for themselves and many of them won't hesitate to rub out you or your group in order to get what they want. So if you want to have a '**GOOD TIME**' in life, first learn to **survive** and then learn to grab   whatever good times you can get without being noticed. So be a '**CHAMELEON**'. It survives not by being wild or joining a group but by constantly changing its colour in order to fit in with its background and manages to have a good time without attracting the envy and greed of the vicious animals that surround it.

And that's how you should behave. In other words, learn to survive by not being too different from the people you are mixing with. Blend in, change yourself constantly and don't stand out from the others. Instead, follow the crowd, do whatever they are doing and don't attract attention to yourself by doing suicidal things like disagreeing with them on a '**matter of principle**'. 'Principles' are likely to end up with you being hurt, so drop them and concentrate on surviving the day.

For example, if you find yourself amongst racists, don't start mouthing off about '**ALL HUMANS BEING OF EQUAL VALUE**.' That will simply make you a target. Instead, adopt their attitudes, their lifestyle and their racist slogans.

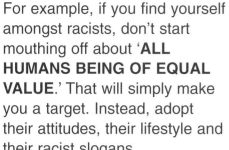

So, Rupert, you want to be a mercenary as well?

And if you find yourself in a class where most of the other kids have no interest in learning but spend their time having a go at the teacher, avoiding homework and ignoring books, then don't start acquiring a reputation for being a swot. Instead, blend in, join in and – like the others – opt out.

And furthermore, if you find yourself amongst kids who spend most of their time on things like 'looking good', partying, and combing their hair, then don't get a reputation for being 'stuck up', a 'snob' or a 'dipstick.' Concentrate on fitting in and doing what they expect you to do. If you don't, then, like a budgie amongst a flock of sparrows, you'll be pecked and eaten alive.

But this is the philosophy of the coward!

Well of course, you're right, but think for a moment, of those people in history who weren't cowards, who didn't blend in with the crowd and who took some sort of stand against the wild animals of this world.

A man called **Steve Biko**, for example, stood up against the racist 'wild animals' of South Africa, but within a very short time he was beaten to a pulp by the security forces and left to die in the back of a truck.

There was also a man called **Deitrich Bonhoeffer**. He refused to let the 'animals' called Nazis push him around and he ended up hanging from a rope by the neck.

And then there was an Italian magistrate called **Carlo Alberto Dalla Chiesa** who took on the 'animals' called 'The Mafia'. They had him and his young wife blown to pieces.

So don't knock 'cowards.' At least they tend to survive in this world (unlike the brave) and you can't have a '**GOOD TIME**' in life unless you manage that.

1 The boy in this section also believes that the best way to enjoy life is to live a self-centred life. He believes that the best way to do this is to live the life of a 'chameleon'. Explain his point of view.

2 The girl on page 20 disagrees with this advice. Explain her reasons for doing so.

3 Explain his reply to these objections in your own words.

4 Have you ever behaved like a 'chameleon'? Give details or reasons why not.

5 Do you think that you should abandon all your principles when your survival is at stake, or do you think that in some circumstances 'death' can be preferable to 'life?' Give reasons for your answer.

6 A well known proverb says, 'It is better to live one day as a lion than a hundred years as a sheep'.

(a) What do you think this means?

(b) Do you agree with its meaning?

7 Why do you think that Steve Biko, Deitrich Bonhoeffer and Carlo Alberto Dalla Chiesa were not prepared to live like chameleons?

8 Do you like yourself more when you don't behave like a chameleon? Give reasons for your answer.

RESEARCH

9 Research the lives of either Steve Biko, Deitrich Bonhoeffer or Carlo Alberto Dalla Chiesa.

THE WOLF CHILDREN

At the beginning of this century two young girls called Kamala and Amala lost contact with their parents and were adopted by a mother wolf. The girls grew up surrounded by wolves, took on their identity and spent their childhood doing all the things that make wolves happy. But, since they possessed none of the wolves' abilities to run, fight or hunt, it was clear to those who found the girls that their lives as wolves had been a frightening, brutal and depressing experience.

In 1920 they were discovered by the Rev J.A.L. Singh, who had been asked to exorcise a 'man ghost' that was frightening local villagers and which turned out to be Kamala and Amala, who emerged snarling from a cave with their mother wolf and two other cubs. The mother wolf was killed and the two girls rescued and reintroduced to human beings. Although both girls stopped walking on all fours and began to eat food other than raw meat, they never understood that they were human beings and so were never able to understand the life they ought to be living in order to enjoy it fully. They both died within a few years of their rescue.

Many religious people would say that there are people in this world who can't enjoy life because they have similar problems to these wolf children.

What's that supposed to mean?

Well, Kamala and Amala had no idea what it meant to be a **HUMAN BEING**, so they took on the false identity of a wolf and ended up trying (unsuccessfully) to be happy living a life that was '**inhuman**'.

Many religious people will say that, in the same sort of way there are many people who have no idea what it means to be a **REAL HUMAN BEING**. They also then take on false identities of animals like 'wild dogs', 'pigs,' 'gorillas' and 'chameleons' and so, like the wolf children, end up trying to be happy living **INHUMAN LIVES**.

Religious people then say that the only way we can have a good time in life is if we stop adopting the lifestyles of animals and start **to behave** as a **HUMAN BEING** ought to behave.

So how should a human being behave?

Well, in the next section of this book we will be looking at what the religions **Hinduism** and **Christianity** say you must do if you want to stop behaving like an animal and live and enjoy the life of a real human being.

1　In your own words, explain the problems of Kamala and Amala.

2　Some religious people say that those who live like 'dogs', 'pigs', 'gorillas' or 'chameleons' have the same sort of problems in life as Kamala and Amala. Explain.

3　What, according to these people, is the solution to these problems?

HINDUISM
AND
THE BATTLE TO BE HUMAN

Amala and Kamala couldn't be happy in this world because they
thought they were wolves. Hindus will tell you that human beings
find it difficult to be happy in this world because they identify with
a thing called a '**SELF**' and that this belief in a '**self**' encourages
many to live the **self**-centred lives of 'dogs', 'pigs', 'gorillas' and
'chameleons'. According to Hindus, however, this thing we call
my**self** doesn't actually exist and is not what we are. Those then
that live **self**-centred lives are living (like Kamala and Amala) in
a world of illusion, so they can't possibly enjoy life fully. This
chapter will explain this idea in more detail.

ILLUSIONS

In your science lessons you have probably been taught that you don't actually '**see**' with your eyes. The eyes are simply aerials which pick up light signals and send them in electrical form to the brain. The brain then, like a television receiver, tries to turn these electrical signals into a picture. However, on occasions the brain has problems with the signals and will give us a picture of something which isn't actually there.

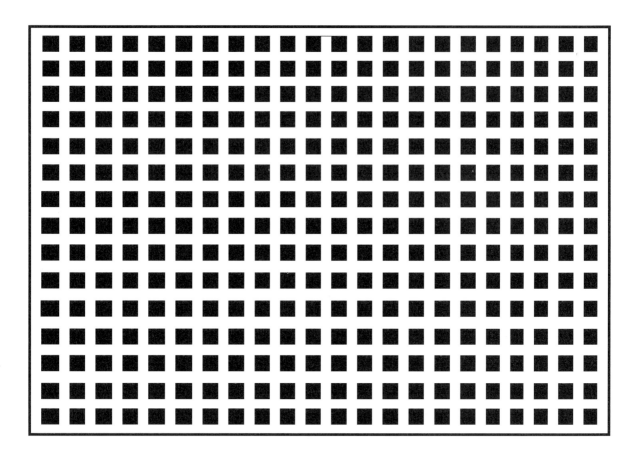

Look for example at the picture above. If you stare at it for a while you will begin to see grey circles appearing at the edges of each of the boxes. Of course, the circles don't actually exist. They are **ILLUSIONS** created by your brain because it is unable to understand the electrical signals coming to it via your eyes.

Now, Hindus believe that when we look at the world (and not just pictures of squares) our brain, once again, doesn't give us an accurate picture of what is there. Instead it gives us a picture of an entire world that doesn't actually exist – '**A WORLD OF TOTAL ILLUSION.**'

What illusions are you talking about?

Well, first of all, when we look at the world we see it as containing lots of '**DIFFERENT SOLID OBJECTS**' (like trees, flowers, rocks, stones etc.), Furthermore, we see our**selves** as being different to these objects because:

(a) We each seem to have a line around us (which we call our shape) and which separates us from these objects.

I hope you've got something to say for yourself!

No self–responsibility whatsoever.

(b) We also seem to have a thing inside of us called a '**self**' (that we call '**me**') and which these objects don't seem to have.

And secondly, when we look at the world we see it as containing lots of '**DIFFERENT PEOPLE**' who are different from our '**selves**' because:

(a) We all seem to have '**different solid shapes**' (i.e. bodies) which separate us from each other;

I'll look after myself and you look after yourself

(b) We all seem to have within us '**different individual selves**' (to which we give different names like Sharon, Khalid and Bert) which once more convinces us that we are separate from each other.

Now, Hindus believe that this picture we have of '**separate**' objects and people is (like the grey dots in the picture) an illusion. They say that the 'lines around us' (which we call shapes) and the '**individual selves**' are not in fact real and are simply the way our brain sees the world. Instead, Hindus believe that beneath the illusion of '**separateness**' all objects and people are part of the same '**SELF**' (which they call either **God**, **Brahman** or **Atman**) and that therefore we are all one with each other.

> 1   Hindus believe that most human beings are living in a world of total illusion. Explain in detail the illusions they believe we see.

I'm not sure I really understand this Hindu idea that we all are 'one' because we are all part of the 'same' self.

Well, one Hindu father tried to help his own son understand this difficult idea in the following way:

When Svetaketu, at his father's bidding, had brought a ripe fruit from the banyam tree, his father said to him,

'Split the fruit in two, dear son.'

'Here you are I have split the fruit in two.'

'What do you find there?'

'Innumerable tiny seeds.'

'Then take one of the seeds and split it.'

'I have split the seed.'

'And what do you find there?'

'Why nothing, nothing at all.'

*'Ah dear son, but this great tree cannot possibly come from nothing. Even if you cannot see with your eyes that subtle something in the seed which produces this mighty form, it is present nonetheless, that is the power, that is the spirit unseen, which pervades everywhere and is in all things. Have faith! That is the spirit which lies at the root of all existence, **AND THAT ALSO ART THOU, O SVETAKETU.'***

The father is then saying that there are no differences between all the created 'things' of **NATURE** (e.g. trees, plants and rocks), **OTHER PEOPLE** and **YOU** because 'at the root' of all things is the same **SPIRITUAL SELF** (i.e. God or Brahman or Atman). Furthermore, he is saying that this spiritual self doesn't simply live *in* a flower, in you or in me, but *is* the flower, *is* you and me (**'and that also art thou, O Svetaketu'**). This **SPIRITUAL SELF**, then, is everything, and everything is the **SPIRITUAL SELF**.

It is like salt dissolved in water for just as the salt cannot be separated from the water and its taste is everywhere within the water, so this **SPIRITUAL SELF (GOD)** is spread throughout everything and cannot be separated from the 'things' it is within. One of the Hindu holy books puts the idea in this way:

One moon or two?

'The soul of all creatures is one soul, but it is also present in every creature; unity and plurality at the same time, like the reflection of the moon on the water.'

Now, this means that Hindus try not to live like the 'dog', 'pig', 'gorilla' and 'chameleon' who always ask '**What's in it for me?**' before they do anything. That's because Hindus believe that there isn't a 'thing' called an individual '**ME**' which is in competition with other '**ME's.**' Instead, they try to live **ALTRUISTICALLY**, i.e. not elevating the thing we call '**me**' above others but living in the understanding that '**me**' and '**you**' are '**one**' with needs that have the same value.

1   Explain why Hindus try not to live the self-centred lives of 'dogs', 'pigs', 'gorillas' and 'chameleons'.

2   The story in this section says that Hindus believe that there are no differences between the '**things**' **of nature**, **other people** and **you**. Explain.

3   Try to think of your own way of expressing the Hindu idea of 'oneness' either through a poem, a drawing or an explanation.

4   What does '**to live altruistically**' mean?

DYING TO LIVE: MAHATMA GANDHI

'I must reduce myself to zero. So long as a man does not of his own free will put himself last amongst his fellow creatures, there is no salvation (from the illusion) for him.'

Many Hindus will tell you that if you want to see Hinduism in action you should look at the life of a man called Mahatma Gandhi. He was a man, they say, who took seriously the view that all human beings share the same '**self**' and are therefore '**one**' with each other. He therefore spent his life opposing the wild animals of this world who lived **self**-centred lives and who constantly tried to elevate them**selves** above other people. And he did this by siding with the people around him who were poor, picked on and those who, in the eyes of '**the elevated ones**', just didn't count for very much. More importantly, Gandhi sided with them without being violent. His idea was to melt his opponents' hearts with love, for his aim was not simply to beat and   humiliate but ultimately to be reconciled even with those who oppress others.

For example:

In South Africa (where he lived for 21 years) many white people in that country regarded the blacks as inferior. The '**Black Laws**' were passed which made them pay more tax than the whites and which said that only Christian marriages were legal (thus making all Indian non-Christian women   mistresses).

One day Gandhi himself was thrown out of a first class carriage on a train because he was breaking the rule that all dark skinned people should travel third class.

Gandhi decided to try and stop this unfair treatment. He also decided it should be done without violence and declared that the whites must be '**WEANED FROM ERROR BY PATIENCE AND SYMPATHY**'. And so when the white-led army and police insulted, flogged and arrested the protesters (a quarter of all Indians were arrested) there was no retaliation. Instead, Gandhi encouraged the protesters to resist peacefully and to respond with patience, concern and love for their oppressors. The white government finally admitted defeat and the 'Black Laws' were repealed.

Later, Gandhi returned to India. There, as in South Africa, he discovered people who spent a great deal of their time elevating them**selves** above others.

The British, for example, who ruled India at this time, often treated the Indian people as if they were inferior to them**selves.** Now, many Indians thought that the British should leave India and let the Indians rule themselves. Gandhi thought so as well, and declared that 'we will make them leave our country **NOT BY FIGHTING WITH THEM, BUT SIMPLY BY REFUSING TO OBEY THE LAWS THEY MAKE**.'

Once again then, Gandhi sided with those who were treated as if they didn't count and organised them into peaceful protests against the British government. He called for a General Strike, a boycott of British goods and urged Indian soldiers in the British army to desert their posts and those Indians who worked for the British government to give up their jobs.

The British responded by firing on a peaceful demonstration killing hundreds of people and imprisoning Gandhi for six years. But once again, he refused to urge his followers to retaliate with violence. Instead, he held to his principle that the oppressors can only truly be conquered with the weapon of love. Like the whites in South Africa, the British were eventually defeated and on August 15th 1945, India became an independent country.

Gandhi also discovered that, within the Indian community itself, there were **'SELF'** important Indians who elevated them**selves** above others. For example, there was a group of people within India called **'the untouchables'** (poor peasants and factory workers) who were treated as if they didn't matter. Gandhi hated the way other Hindus treated these people. He saw it as a complete contradiction of the Hindu belief that we are all part of the same **'self'** and called for the liberation of **the untouchables**. He said they were the **'Children of God'** and refused to worship in temples that kept untouchables out. He accepted and identified with the untouchables and spent much of his time amongst them.

Now, there were many **'WILD DOGS'** who warned Gandhi that it was in his **'self'**-interest to back off, not to get involved and to behave like a 'chameleon'. But Gandhi refused to be frightened into submission by their threats because he believed that a human life should not be powered by **self**-interest and that to live like that would be '**inhuman**'.

On January 30th 1948, the **'WILD DOGS'** got to Gandhi and he was shot dead by a fellow Hindu.

However, according to many Hindus, this was not the end of Gandhi. Nehru, the Indian Prime Minister, summed up their thoughts in these words:

'The light has gone out' I said, yet I was wrong. For the light that shone in this country was no ordinary light. The light that has illumined this country for this many years will illumine this country for many more years, and a thousand years later that light will be seen in this country, and the world will see it and it will give solace to innumerable hearts. For that light represented the living truth, and the eternal man was with his eternal truth reminding us of the right path, drawing us from the error, taking this ancient country to freedom.

1 In your own words explain how Gandhi put into practice the Hindu belief that we all share the 'same' self. Answer this question by giving some details of his work in South Africa and India.

2 Why did Gandhi refuse to live the self-centred life of either a 'wild dog', 'pig', 'gorilla' or 'chameleon'?

3 Gandhi ended up getting shot. Some would say that this demonstrates why a selfless life is the worst type of life to lead. How might a Hindu reply to this view?

4 Some people say that 'You shouldn't judge a life by its length but by its quality'. Do you agree? Give reasons for your answer.

5 Nehru, the Indian Prime Minister, said that the death of Gandhi was not the end of him, i.e. the light of Gandhi's life 'represented the living truth'. What do you think he meant? Do you agree?

RESEARCH

6 Investigate what Hindus believe about life after death by researching the following:

(a) karma

(b) reincarnation

(c) moksha.

CHRISTIANITY
AND THE BATTLE TO BE HUMAN

The religion of Christianity also says that the reason we all have problems having a 'good time' in life is that like the Wolf Children, we have an '**identity problem**.' However, unlike Hinduism, Christianity says that the individual self is REAL. The problem then is not that we identify with an ILLUSION Instead it is that we identify with a **MAGNIFIED** view of a real self. Christians say it is this **DISTORTION** which encourages us to live the '**self**'-centred lives of either 'dogs', 'pigs', 'gorillas' or 'chameleons'. This chapter will try to explain this idea in more detail.

A DISTORTED VIEW OF THE SELF

Think for a moment of those occasions when you have gone to a travelling fairground with your family or friends and paid money to stand in front of a variety of wonky mirrors. Suddenly, you become hideously **DISTORTED**, with arms lengthened, legs shortened, your trunk squashed and your head twisted into a variety of different shapes.

Now, you know, of course, that the image in the mirror is not a total illusion (like a mirage) for you recognise that the '**being**' in the mirror actually exists and that this 'being' is '**YOU**'. However, you also recognise that the reflection is a **DISTORTION** and is thankfully (or hopefully) not an accurate reflection of what you really look like.

Now, Christianity says that the reason we all have problems enjoying life fully is that when we look at (or understand) our**selves** and other '**selves**' in life, the images we see are totally **distorted** and that (unlike the fairground mirrors), we actually believe that these images are an accurate reflection of what is there.

I'm not sure I understand what you're talking about.

Well, Christianity says that when we look at ourselves we tend to 'see' or understand our**selves** as **GIANTS** occupying enormous amounts of space in the landscape and so enormously **self**-important. We see then our needs, wants, desires, interests, worries, problems, insecurities and happiness as being **GIGANTICALLY IMPORTANT**. So we spend a great deal of our time gazing at our**selves**, thinking about our**selves**, worrying about our**selves** and pleasing our**selves**. In other words, living (like 'dogs', 'pigs', 'gorillas' and 'chameleons') **self**-centred existences that go through life looking after number one and asking questions like **'What's in it for me?'**.

We also tend to 'see' other '**selves**' as **DWARFS** occupying minute amounts of space in the landscape and so next to our**selves** enormously unimportant. We spend little time, then, looking beyond our own gigantic noses at these other '**selves**'. Their needs, wants, desires, interests, worries, problems, insecurities and happiness seem **minutely** unimportant next to our own. So they often fade away into nothing in the shadow of the thing we call '**ME**'.

Now the religion of Christianity says that if you want to enjoy life fully then you will need to 'see' (or understand) your**self** and other **selves** as you really are and that this can best be achieved if you are prepared to look in an **UNDISTORTED MIRROR** made by God. This mirror, say Christians, is called '**The BIBLE**' and has been given to us by our Creator so that we can 'see' our**selves** and each other as we really are.

1 Like Hinduism, Christianity says that the reason why we have problems enjoying life fully is that we have an 'identity problem'. However, the Christian explanation of this problem does not appear to be the same as the Hindu one. Explain the differences.

2 Christianity says that we tend to see ourselves as **giants** and other selves as **dwarfs**. Explain what this means and whether it is true of you.

3 To investigate your own (possible) self-centred life draw a bar graph indicating what you spend your money on each week (e.g. clothes, cds etc.). The graph should also indicate how much of your spending is on yourself and how much is on other people.

RESEARCH

4 (a) Find out what Ptolemy (a 2nd-century astronomer) and Copernicus (a 16th-century astronomer) said was at the centre of the universe.

(b) Some people say that we have problems enjoying life because we find it difficult to leave our own personal Ptolemaic universe and move to one that is more Copernican. Explain what you think this might mean. Do you agree?

(c) Draw a picture of your 'self' at the centre of your universe with various people in orbit around you. Indicate who these people might be.

So how does this mirror (the Bible) encourage us to see ourselves?

Don't overestimate yourself

Well first of all, Christians will say that when you look into God's mirror, the Bible, you see yourself next to God and your own size immediately shrinks. You are no longer a giant occupying large amounts of space in the landscape. Instead, God is the giant and your **self**-importance is **dwarfed** by his power, intelligence and wisdom. This, of course, makes it difficult for you (or anybody) to go through life living **self**-centred lives, elevating your**self** above other '**selves**' and generally living as if you were the most important object in the universe with all the **GIGANTIC** knowledge and wisdom required to live a happy life. Instead, you begin to see your**self** in perspective and to recognise how small you are in the landscape. One writer in the Bible makes this idea clear in a conversation between God and a man called Job:

God *Who are you to question my wisdom with your ignorant empty words? Were you there when I made the world? If you know so much, tell me about it. Who decided how large it would be? Do you know all the answers? Do you know where the light comes from or the source of darkness? Do you know the laws that govern the skies, and can you shout orders to the clouds and make them drench you with rain? And if you command the lightning to flash will it come to you and say 'At your service'? Was it you, Job, who made horses so strong and gave them flowing manes? Did you make them leap like locusts? Does a hawk learn from you how to fly when it spreads its wings towards the south? Job, you challenged Almighty God; will you give up now, or will you answer?*

Job *I know Lord, that you are all powerful, that you can do everything you want. You ask how I dare question your wisdom when I am so very ignorant. I talked about things I did not understand, about marvels too great for me to understand. I am ashamed of all I have said and repent.*

Don't underestimate others (or yourself)

Secondly, Christians will tell you that in God's mirror your new vision of your**self** makes it impossible for you to see the other '**selves**' around you as '**dwarfs**'. You are no longer head and shoulders above anybody. Your needs, wants, desires, interests, worries, problems, insecurities and happiness are no longer seen as being more important than those that surround you. And because others emerge from the shadow of the the thing you call '**ME**' you no longer see them as rival 'dogs', 'pigs', 'gorillas' or 'chameleons'. Instead, you begin to recognise them as '**family**'. For in God's mirror it becomes increasingly clear that you are all '**Children of God**' and that others are your long lost brothers and sisters.

In God's mirror then, Christians do not see the world as a jungle, other people as rival wild animals and life as a competition where the winners are those who look after number one and always ask '**What's in it for me?**'. Instead, Christians see the world as a place that can be like **heaven** and life as an opportunity to achieve this heaven by living lives which are **ALTRUISTIC** and which care for one another as '**family**'.

1 Christians will tell you that, if you want to see a true reflection of yourself and others, you should look in a mirror provided by God .

   (a) Explain what they mean by 'God's Mirror'.

   (b) Explain what new things they believe we will see about **the world**, **ourselves** and **others**.

2 When you look at the **world**, **yourself** and **others** do you tend to see what Christians say you should see? Give reasons for your answer.

DYING TO LIVE: JESUS CHRIST

'If anyone wants to come with me', he told them 'he must forget himself, carry his cross, and follow me. For whoever wants to save his own life will lose it; but whoever loses his life for me and for the gospel will save it. Does a man gain anything if he wins the whole world but loses his own life? Of course not!'

Christians will tell you that if you want to see Christianity in action then you should look at the life of a man called Jesus. This man, they say, took seriously the view that we all share the same heavenly father and are   therefore all brothers and sisters with equal value in the sight of God. Like Gandhi, Jesus refused to live the **self**-centred life of either a 'dog', 'pig', 'gorilla' or 'chameleon'. Instead, he always opposed those who were   puffed up with **self**-importance and who tried to elevate them**selves** above others by constantly siding with those people who, in the eyes of '**the elevated ones**', just didn't count for very much. Like Gandhi, his opposition was never violent for his idea was also to melt his opponents' hearts with love and ultimately to be reconciled with them.

For example:

The sick and handicapped

At the time of Jesus many believed that sickness was either a punishment from God for your sins or because you were possessed by evil demons. Many **self**-important people, then, looked down on physically and mentally sick people and would have nothing to do with them. They were shunned and turned into social out-casts. Jesus, however, totally rejected the idea that the sick were in some way responsible for their sickness and should therefore be despised. He simply saw them as '**Children of God**' in need of health, strength and hope and so cared for them as brothers and sisters.

The poor

Poverty, too, was regarded by many as a sign that God was not on your side. Therefore, many '**self**'-important rich people looked down on the deprived, the failures, the powerless, and the insignificant as sinners who deserved all they got. However, Jesus rejected the idea that the poor were evil who deserved their raw deal. Again, he saw them as '**Children of God**' in need of acceptance. Jesus then went out of his way to identify himself with these 'little' people.

For example, he chose as his disciples those whom many regarded as uneducated, ignorant, backward and immoral. He mixed socially with those that others had written off and claimed that the message he had brought from God was '**GOOD NEWS FOR THE POOR.**'

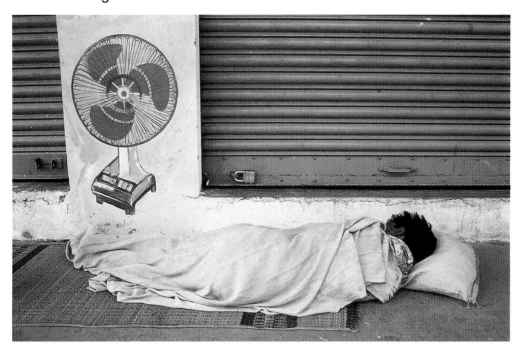

The immoral

Many **self**-important people (as they do today) separated them**selves** totally from the so-called hopeless, immoral and irreligious people that lived within their communities. They built their houses as far away as possible from the hovels they lived in, avoided walking near their communities and refused to have anything to do with them. Jesus, however, simply saw them as '**Children of God**' and outraged many 'respectable' people by the way he got involved with these 'low-lifes'. He spent much of his time in the company of so-called drunks, down-and-outs, cheats, swindlers, pimps and prostitutes and seemed to have got on very well with them. Not because he did what they did, but because he accepted them, sat with them, talked to them and cared for them as brothers and sisters and not as a professional carer.

The rich exploiters

Jesus showed no hatred towards those who exploited the poor. He refused to look down on them as '**the filthy rich**', to isolate himself from them (as some revolutionaries suggested) or to encourage revenge, revolution or the oppression of the oppressor. Instead, he saw them as '**Children of God**' who needed help to be liberated from their love of money. So he accepted invitations from rich priests and rich tax collectors, and actually chose a tax collector to be one of his special disciples. He accepted them, sat with them, told them that wealth was dangerous and encouraged them to see that the poor who surrounded them were their brothers and sisters.

Now, as with Gandhi, there were many '**WILD DOGS**' who warned Jesus that it was in his **self**- interest not to be such a troublemaker and to adopt the conformist attitude of a 'chameleon'. However, like Gandhi, he refused to be frightened into submission by their threats for he believed that a human life should not be powered by **self**-interest because to live like that would be '**inhuman**'.

At the age of 33 the '**WILD DOGS**' got to Jesus. He was betrayed by a close companion, subsequently arrested, beaten up and tortured while in custody, found guilty of stirring up the people and finally nailed to a cross to suffer a deliberately slow and agonising death.

However, as with Gandhi, many believe that this was not the end of Jesus. A man called Paul, who was an early follower of Jesus, has summed up their thoughts in the following way:

'And now I want to remind you, my brothers, of the good news which I received, and on which your faith stands firm ... that Christ died for our sins, as written in the Scriptures, that he was buried and that he was raised to life three days later, as written in the Scriptures, that he appeared to Peter and then to all twelve apostles. Then he appeared to more than five hundred of his followers at once ... Then he appeared to James ... last of all he appeared to me ...
If our hope in Christ is good for this life only and no more, then we deserve more pity than anyone else in all the world. But the truth is that Christ has been raised from death, as the guarantee that those who sleep in death will also be raised.'
(I Corinthians 15:1-8, 18-20)

1 What kinds of people were looked down upon during the times of Jesus? Explain why.

2 What was Jesus' attitude toward these people? Explain why.

3 Jesus refused to live the self-centred life of either a 'wild dog', 'pig', 'gorilla' or 'chamelon'. Explain his reasons.

4 Jesus ended up being killed by the 'wild dogs' of this world. Some would say that this is an overwhelming reason to ignore the advice of Jesus to live a selfless life. What do you think? Give reasons for your answer.

5 Do you think that a 'short selfless life' is more satisfying and enjoyable than a 'long selfish life'? Give reasons for your answer.

6 The writer called Paul did not believe that the death of Jesus was the end of Jesus. Explain his views.

7 Christians claim that life is a journey that continues beyond the grave and that each of us will have to answer to God for the life we have chosen to lead. Do you agree? Give reasons for your answer.